The Kids' Book of Prayers about All Sorts of Things

by Elizabeth Heller and
David Heller, Ph.D.

Pauline
BOOKS & MEDIA
Boston

Nihil Obstat: Very Rev. Timothy J. Shea, V. F.
Imprimatur: Bernard Cardinal Law
                 June 21, 1994

                 Library of Congress Cataloging-in-Publication Data
Heller, Elizabeth.
  The kids' book of prayers about all sorts of things / by Elizabeth Heller and
David Heller.
     p.   cm.
  ISBN 0-8198-4200-1 (pbk.)
  1. Children—Prayer-books and devotions—English. 2. Prayers—Juvenile literature.
[1. Prayer books and devotions. 2. Prayers.] I. Heller, David. II. Title.
BV265.H39 1994
242' .82—dc20   94-26559
                                                 CIP
                                                 AC

Photo credits: *M. Emmanuel Alves, FSP:* pp. 10 (both), 11 (both), 32 (top), 33 (top),
56 (both), 76 (both), 77 (top), 92 (top), 93 (both), 120 (top), 121 (top)
Daughters of St. Paul: pp. 32 (bottom), 33 (bottom), 77 (bottom), 92 (bottom)
Rebecca Horton, O.P.: p. 121 (bottom)
Natick Recreation & Park Dept.: p. 120 (bottom),
Linda Smith: p. 57 (both)

Illustrations by: *Megan Jeffery:* pp. 37, 42, 48, 108, 136
                   Kathryn Mitter: pp. 23, 46, 50, 60, 99

Published in the U.S.A. by Pauline Books & Media, 50 Saint Pauls Avenue, Boston
MA 02130-3491.

Printed in the U.S.A.

www.pauline.org

KBP VSAUSAPEOILL05-10J10-03727 4200-1

Pauline Books & Media is the publishing house of the Daughters of St. Paul, an international congregation of women religious serving the Church with the communications media.

7 8 9 10 11   14 13 12 11 10

To our dear friend,
Catherine Masterson

This book belongs to

_____

TABLE OF CONTENTS

Introduction 9

Chapter 1   Prayers of Thankfulness 11
A Prayer about My Parents 12
A Prayer about Grandparents 14
A Prayer about Brothers and Sisters 16
Gratitude for a Helpful Teacher 18
A Prayer about a Good Friend 20
Thankfulness for the Earth 22
Offering Before a Meal 24
The Quiet Time Prayer 26
A Prayer about Good Health 28
Having Food, Clothing and Shelter 30

Chapter 2   Prayers Asking God for Help 33
On Misbehavior at Home 34
When You're Having a Hard Day 36
A Prayer about the First Day of School 38
Help with Homework 40
Trouble with Other Kids at School 42
Feeling for Others 44
Listening to Teachers and Other Adults 46
Making New Friends 48
Getting Along with All Kinds of People 50
Being Honest 52
When You're Confused about God 54

**Chapter 3   Prayers About
                Everyday Feelings** 57
Laughter 58
When You Feel Afraid 60
Happiness 62
Feeling Sad 64
On Love 66
On Being Angry 68
Feeling Silly 70
About Loneliness 72
Sharing 74

Chapter 4 Prayers About Things that Happen in Our World 77

A Prayer for the Homeless 78
A Prayer about Schools and Learning 80
The Drug Problem 82
Prejudice 84
On the Environment 86
About Crime 88
A Prayer for Our National Leaders 90

Chapter 5 Prayers About All Kinds of Things 93

Help with Solving a Problem 94
On Judging Other People 96
Asking for Forgiveness 98
When You Make a Mistake 100
Growing Up with One Parent 102
A Get Well Wish for Someone You Love 104
When a Grandparent Dies 106
A Graduation Prayer 108
A Prayer for a Safe Journey or Vacation 110
Love for a Pet 112
When a Pet Dies 114
About Playing Sports 116
About the Bible 118

Chapter 6 Prayers About Holidays and Special Times 121

A Birthday Prayer 122
A Prayer for the New Year 124
A Prayer for Martin Luther King Day 126
For Valentine's Day 128
For President's Day 130
An Easter/Springtime Prayer 132
About the Fourth of July 134
Halloween 136
A Prayer for Thanksgiving 138
A Christmas Prayer 140

About the Authors 142
A Word to Parents and Teachers 143

INTRODUCTION

God is always there to listen to us and to help us. But sometimes we may not be sure of the best way to share our thoughts and feelings with God. Praying is a wonderful way to talk to God. And the best thing about prayer is that there are all kinds of ways to pray.

This is a book that will help you explore different ways to pray about all different subjects. The fun part is that there is no right or wrong way to pray. All you need is a sincere heart and your imagination and your belief in God.

As you go through the pages of this book you will find prayers about things like playing sports or having a best friend. There are prayers about holidays like Christmas and Halloween. You'll also find prayers about the environment and social problems like drugs and homelessness.

Following each prayer is a suggestion as to how you might pray about the particular topic. You can try this suggestion or make up your own way of praying about the subject. You may want to get ideas from your teacher or parents as well.

Sometimes where you pray can be important. Maybe you are most comfortable at church, or in your room or outside under a favorite tree. Or maybe you like to pray in the kitchen while dinner is being pre-pared. Some people like to choose a special place they call "a prayer corner." You can turn any quiet place, where you won't be bothered much, into a prayer corner. Spending time in this special place can give you a chance to think about things that are important to you. You can choose to pray wherever you are most comfortable.

The Kids' Book of Prayers About All Sorts of Things is a fun way to talk to God. Prayer is a wonder-ful way to communicate your feelings and thoughts to God and to get to know God better and better. As it says in the Bible: "Whatever you ask for in prayer with faith, you will receive" (Matthew 21:22).

Elizabeth Heller and David Heller, Boston

Chapter 1

Prayers of Thankfulness

"Lord how I love you, for you have done
such tremendous things for me"
(cf. Psalm 18:1).

A Prayer about My Parents

God, I'm really thankful for my parents.
You have blessed me with a
really good mom and dad.
They are there for me when I have a problem
and they help me with difficult things.
I like to talk with them
and sometimes they can be funny, too.
They want me to learn a lot in school
and they encourage me
and support me all the time,
even if I don't always succeed in things I try.
I know they love me, God.
And that's the best part of all.
Thank you, God, for giving me such good
parents.

☞ Now write your own original prayer about your parents.
What would you especially like to say to God about your
parents? Take some time out to talk with God about
these most important people in your life.

A Prayer about Grandparents

My grandparents make me feel special,
God. When I visit them we always
find fun things to do.
My grandmother makes my favorite foods.
My grandfather teaches me about things.
My grandparents love me a lot, God.
And I'm so happy that they are here
to spend time with.
They tell me funny stories about
my mom and dad
and it makes me laugh.
Thank You for my grandparents, God.
And please bless them so I can be with them
for a long, long time.

☞ What do you enjoy most about your grandparents? Now write a
letter to God about your grandparent or grandparents. Tell God
what they mean to you. Then write a letter directly to a
grandparent and tell them how you feel. Grandparents always
appreciate letters or notes from their grandchildren.

Dear God,

Love,

Dear _____,

Love,

15

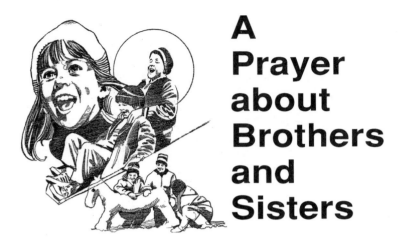

A Prayer about Brothers and Sisters

God, thank you for my brother(s) and
sister(s). Even though we fight sometimes,
I really like having them around.
It's nice to have someone to
play with and talk with.
I learn things about life from them, too.
They always support me
when I am competing at things
or trying to accomplish something at school.
And they cheer me up
when I don't do so well at something.
I think they are proud of me
and I know I am proud of them.
Thank you, Lord,
for my brother(s) and sister(s).

☞ Do you have a brother or sister? What do you like about having
them in the family? Now think of something nice to do for your
brother or sister and let that be your prayer to God about him or
her. (You may want to use this space to put down ideas about
the things you can do for your brother or sister.)

①

②

③

④

17

Gratitude for a Helpful Teacher

God, thank you for my teacher.
It's very nice to have someone
who helps me with my schoolwork
and makes learning fun.
We do interesting things in my class,
and my teacher never makes me feel silly
for asking a question.
I know my teacher cares about me
and about what I learn.
Thank you so much, God.
My teacher is a wonderful instructor.

☞ Is there a teacher or adult in your life who is helpful to
you? What does that person do to give you support and
help? Write an original prayer about a teacher or other
adult in your life who helps you in a special way.

A Prayer about a Good Friend

I'd like to say a special prayer for a
good friend of mine.
My friend always helps me
when I'm confused or when I need
extra help on my homework.
We play together and share secrets, too.
And we never run out of things to talk about.
We try to help each other with everything,
like schoolwork and worries and growing up.
I never feel alone knowing that I have
such a helpful friend.
I feel lucky.
Thank you God, for giving me
such a good friend.

☞ What makes your friend special to you? Design a logo along with your friend that symbolizes your friendship. If you have the necessary materials, develop a T-shirt with the logo on it. Then you will have a permanent symbol of this important friendship.

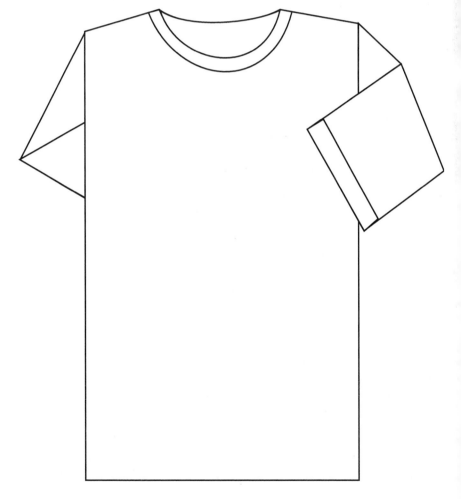

Thankfulness for the Earth

God, I just want to say thank you
for creating such a beautiful world.
I think it's really neat how you made
different seasons.
I love how the sun makes me feel
warm and cheery
and how sometimes, on rainy days,
I feel thoughtful and cozy.
I wonder how you made the clouds and flowers
and so many kinds of animals?
I wonder how you made the stars and sun
above us?
There is so much to know about the earth
and our environment:
I am thankful for all you have given us
and for the curiosity to explore them all.
The earth is a really beautiful creation
and I say these words with joy:
"Oh Lord, ...how majestic is your name
in all the earth!" (Psalm 8:9)

☞ What do you particularly love about the earth? Show God your thankfulness for the earth by planting a small tree or some flowers in your yard. Make it your special offering to care for the plants and help them to grow and flourish.

Offering Before a Meal

I appreciate the fact that breakfast,
lunch and dinner are always there for us.
What a variety of foods you have created,
God! Help me to remember all of the people
involved in getting food to us.
Thank you for the farmers
and the grocery stores.
I promise not to waste food
or eat more than I need.
And please bless all of those people
who don't have enough food to eat
and help them not to be hungry.
Please look after them, God,
and please help us all to share with them.
Amen.

☞ Now write your own original prayer that can be offered before a meal. Then ask your parents if you may prepare part of the meal, and ask to recite your prayer beforehand. Perhaps other family members may want to write their own prayers and share them on the next few evenings.

The Quiet Time Prayer

Sometimes on an afternoon
when no one's home to play,
I don't mind, 'cause it's a quiet time
when my dreams come out and stray.

I go outside and lie on the grass
and watch the clouds in the sky,
and all along I sing a song
and watch grasshoppers go by.

Then I dream about the things
God made for us to do,
like watching flowers in the spring
or snowflakes fresh and new.

And when the clouds have passed
and my dreaming is all through,
I thank the Lord for my quiet time
and the dreams I think of, too.

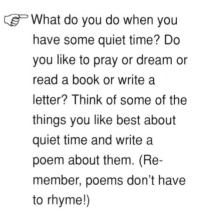

☞ What do you do when you have some quiet time? Do you like to pray or dream or read a book or write a letter? Think of some of the things you like best about quiet time and write a poem about them. (Remember, poems don't have to rhyme!)

A Prayer about Good Health

I am very happy to have good health, God.
Thank you for keeping me safe
from harm and illness.
I feel blessed to be able to play and run and
jump. I know some kids cannot play like me
and some children are very sick
and even in the hospital.
Please God, help these children
to get well soon.
And help me to appreciate
the health I have
and inspire me
to remember
the other children
in my prayers.
Amen.

☞ Think about what you
would like to say to
God about your
health. Now make a
list of ten positive
things you will do to
stay healthy or
improve your health.
Ask God to help you
with the items on
your list.

My Health Plan

1.

2.

3.

4.

5.

6.

7.

8.

9.

10.

Having Food, Clothing and Shelter

God, I'd like to take some time out
and think about how thankful I am
that I have food, clothing and shelter.
Sometimes I take these things for granted
because they are always there.
But I know that I am lucky to have them.
Some people worry every day
about where they will get food
and how they will protect themselves
from the rain and cold.
I am sorry for the times I complain
when I don't get clothes with designer labels
or don't get to eat a lot of candy.
I am thankful that I have the clothes I need,
a nice warm bed and good food.
Please inspire us all to help people
who need these fundamental things.

☞ Think for a moment about our basic needs. Now discuss with your class, your family or your friends what you can do to help people who are needy. Perhaps you can hold a food drive at school or volunteer to help needy people in some other way. Let your actions speak as your heartfelt prayer to God, as you remember that every person is a child of God and worthy of respect and help.

Paste a photo here
showing you
helping needy
people.

Helping the Needy

Chapter 2

Prayers
Asking God for Help

"The Lord is my Shepherd,
I shall not want"
(Psalm 23:1).

On Misbehavior at Home

God, I did something I wasn't supposed to
do. _____ (name the person)
got very mad at me.
I'm really sorry that I did it and
that I didn't listen.
I know that parents make rules
for a good reason
and that they are trying to protect
their children.
I know, God, that there are times
when certain rules have to be broken,
so people can be safe or can be helped.
This was not one of those times.
Please forgive me.
It's hard for me to behave sometimes, God,
so please help me to obey my parents' rules.

☞ How do you feel when you misbehave? Have
you tried to talk to God about it? Write an
original prayer to God about your feelings
concerning misbehavior.

When You're Having a Hard Day

I think it's hard to be real nice
to people every day,
sometimes they make me angry
because they won't let me play.

Sometimes I even see someone
hurting someone else,
and I don't know quite what to do
and I'm quiet as a mouse.

So I ask you, God, to help me
to speak up when I can,
and help someone who's being hurt
by someone else's hand.

And if I do, just maybe
I can help the world along
by spreading a little kindness
because kindness makes us strong.

☞ When is it hard for you to be nice to people? How do you act
when you've had a difficult day and don't feel like being kind?
Now write a poem about tough times. What would you like to
ask God when you're having a hard day? (Remember, poems
don't have to rhyme!)

A Prayer about the First Day of School

God, as you know,
it's the beginning of a new school year.
Thank you for the summer
and all the fun I had.
But help me to remember that
now I have to find time
to do well in school and try my very best.
Please help me to learn
about all kinds of interesting ideas.
Help me to make some new friends
and get along well with my classmates.
And thank you for the fall
and the nice weather.
It helps to make
the beginning of school special.

☞ What do you feel like on the first day of a new school year?
Now make a list of ten things you would like to accomplish this
school year. After you have made the list, write a prayer to God
asking for help with the things on your list. Then put a copy of
the list where you will see it every morning. Each day, read the
list and ask God to help you with your goals.

List

Prayer

Help with Homework

God,
sometimes it is hard
to concentrate on my schoolwork.
There are so many things
I want to do after school.
I like to watch TV and play video games
and be with my friends.
My work is not very good
when I get distracted.
Help me to concentrate better
and to organize my time so
I can get my homework done
and still have time to play.
I know my homework is important
and I want to do well.
With your help, God, I know I can do better.

☞ Do you sometimes ignore your homework to do something like
watch TV? Is there a certain subject that is especially hard for
you? Ask your parents to sit down with you and help you make
an after-school schedule. First, write down those things you do
after school and how much time you spend doing those things.
With your parents help, decide what is most important and
where you can spend your time more wisely. Make a weekly
schedule of how you will spend your after-school hours. Once
you have organized your time, ask God to help you stick to
your schedule each day.

SUNDAY:	MONDAY:

TUESDAY:	WEDNESDAY:

THURSDAY:	FRIDAY:

SATURDAY:	Important this week:

Trouble
with
Other
Kids
at
School

I don't know why kids at school tease me.
It hurts my feelings and makes me angry.
Sometimes I feel like I don't fit in
and it's lonely.
God, please help me not to ever be mean
like some children are to me.
And please help them to see
how much it hurts someone else.
Help the kids to stop teasing me.
Help all children to be kinder people
and help me to get through this rough time.

☞ Have your feelings ever been hurt by kids at
school? Have you ever hurt someone else's
feelings? Now create your own skit or short play
about children hurting other children's feelings.
How can you resolve the problems that being
mean creates? Act out your skit at school or with
your family or friends.

by _____

Cast:

Feeling
for
Others

God,
I see people
who need friends.
Some kids
are overweight
and people make jokes
about them.
Some kids are really smart
and I know other children
who won't let them
into their group.
I think these kids
must feel lonely and left out.
Inspire me to include them in
things that I do,
so they will feel welcome
and liked.

☞ Have you ever felt left out? Have you noticed someone recently who might need some special attention or friendship? As your prayer to God, make a sincere effort to include someone new (or someone you would not normally include) in a game at recess or in some other activity. Try to get to know this person a little better and let them know you care about their feelings.

Listening to Teachers and Other Adults

God,
help me to remember
that adults know things
that I haven't learned yet.
Teachers and other grown-ups have rules
and guidelines for a reason.
And even though it's hard sometimes
to obey them,
guide me so that I do listen
and understand that they
are trying to teach me
things I need to know. Amen.

☞ How do you feel when your teachers set rules and
guidelines for you? Is it easy or hard to obey them?
Now draw a picture of yourself when you are asked to
obey a rule. Write a caption or a few descriptive
words about what is happening in the picture.

Making New Friends

God, it's hard for me to make new friends.
I feel unsure of myself
when I don't know someone.
Sometimes I want to say hello
to someone new,
but I'm afraid that they will ignore me.
Many times I don't even try.
I would like to have some new friends,
God. Will you please help me
not to be afraid to take risks?
Maybe some other kids would like
a new friend, too.

☞ Make a list of qualities that go into being a good friend. Is
there anyone around you right now who has many of these
qualities? Try to get to know them better by striking up a
conversation or eating lunch with them. Remember that all
friendships start with a "hello" and a warm smile.

Getting Along with All Kinds of People

There are people
of many races and religions
in my neighborhood and at my school.
It's like having a rainbow of friends.
But sometimes I hear people making jokes
or saying narrow-minded things about my
friends because they are different.
It makes me feel angry, God.
Please help the children at school
and in my neighborhood
to try harder to love and respect each other.
We are all the same inside.
We are all your children.
Please God, help people to understand
and help us to overcome our prejudices.

☞ Now write an original prayer about your feelings concerning people who are different from you. Is there anything you would especially like to work on with God?

Being Honest

I know being honest is very important, God.
When I tell the truth
it makes me feel good all over.
But it's difficult to be honest all the time,
and once in a while I don't exactly
tell the whole truth.
Sometimes I'm afraid I'll get in trouble
if I'm honest
or I'm afraid I won't fit in with the other kids
if I say how I feel.
Please help me to be strong enough
to always tell the truth.
I know with your help I can be honest and
truthful.

☞ When is it hard for you to tell the truth?
Now write an honest prayer of your own
about times you haven't exactly told the
entire truth. Is there something special you
would like to say to God?

When You're Confused about God

Sometimes you feel so close to me, God,
like you're right inside my heart.
But sometimes I feel like you are far away
and I wonder if you hear my prayers.
I get confused sometimes.
And I hope you won't be mad,
but sometimes it's hard to believe
because you are invisible.
God, help me
to know you better
and help me
to keep believing
even when I am confused
or afraid to believe.

☞ Think of some of the different questions you have
about God. Write down each question and leave
space for an answer. Each day, try to think out an
answer to one question. Ask God to fill your heart with
the answers. Ask God to accompany you during this
important exercise.

I wonder _____ ?

I wonder _____ ?

I wonder _____ ?

I wonder _____ ?

I wonder _____ ?

I wonder _____ ?

I wonder _____ ?

I wonder _____ ?

I wonder _____ ?

I wonder _____ ?

I wonder _____ ?

I wonder _____ ?

Chapter 3

Prayers about Everyday Feelings

"The Lord is my light and my salvation,
whom shall I fear?" (Psalm 27:1)

Laughter

I think you must like
things that are funny, God,
because everyone you created loves to laugh.
I like to hear people laughing.
It makes me feel like laughing, too.
I like how laughter
makes me feel tingly inside.
Somehow laughter brings people
closer together.
Laughter was a great invention, God.
Thanks for giving us things to laugh about!

☞ Get together with some of your friends or
with your family and share stories about
funny things that happened to you. Try to
be aware of how you feel when you laugh
and share your stories.

Put a picture here of you
sharing funny stories
with family or friends.

When You Feel Afraid

When I lie in bed alone at night
and everything's spooky and dark,
I try to remember I'm not alone
and I say a prayer in my heart.

For right inside me, all the time
is all there needs to be,
because I'm never alone, no never alone
because God is always with me.

☞ What kinds of things are you afraid of? Pick something that most frightens you and write a letter to God
explaining your fear. Ask God to help you not to be
so afraid. Remember that God understands our
fears. No fear is too small or silly for God's attention.

DEAR GOD,

Happiness

God, here are some things that make people happy:

- A rainbow after a storm
- Chocolate chip cookies
- Getting a big hug
- When friends remember your birthday
- Getting an A on a test
- Ice skating on a frozen pond
- Sharing secrets with a friend
- Raking leaves for the old man who lives next door
- Dreaming about heaven
- Talking to you, God

There are so many things you have given us that make us feel happy.
Help us always to remember to look for things that make us happy
and thank you for them, too.

☞ Now make a small booklet of things that make you happy. List as many things as you can think of that make you happy. Print them neatly and design a cover and a backcover for your list. You might want to illustrate each one, and then glue or staple the pages together. Now, whenever you feel a little down you can read your book and feel better because the booklet will remind you of what cheers you up!

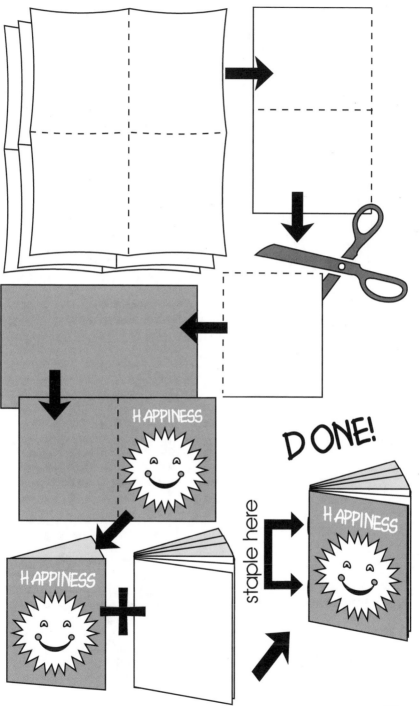

DONE!

staple here

HAPPINESS

HAPPINESS

HAPPINESS

63

Feeling Sad

God, I feel sad once in a while.
Sometimes I feel sad
because someone has hurt my feelings
or treated me unfairly.
Sometimes I feel sad because
I am bored or lonely.
And other times I just feel sad
and I don't know why.
God, when I'm sad I will pray to you
and remember that you are always with me.
I will remember that no matter what,
you always love me.
And I will seek out other
good people to be with.
That will help me feel better.

☞ What makes you feel sad?
Write an original prayer to
God about your feelings.
Make sure you talk to God
about the various things that
bring you down.

On Love

I know that there are lots
of kinds of love, God.
Love is the most wonderful gift
you made for us.
Love is being honest with people
and sharing your feelings with them.
Love is helping a friend to feel happy.
Love is thanking your parents
for how they take care of you and help you.
Love makes your heart tingle
and makes you feel warm on the inside.
Love never seems to end, God.
The more love we give,
the more love grows.
Thank you for loving me, God.
Your love feels the best of all.

☞ Draw a picture of God giving love to the world as a gift. You may also draw a picture of the people you love best. Then draw another picture, but this one will take special thought: have your drawing show how much love you feel for God.

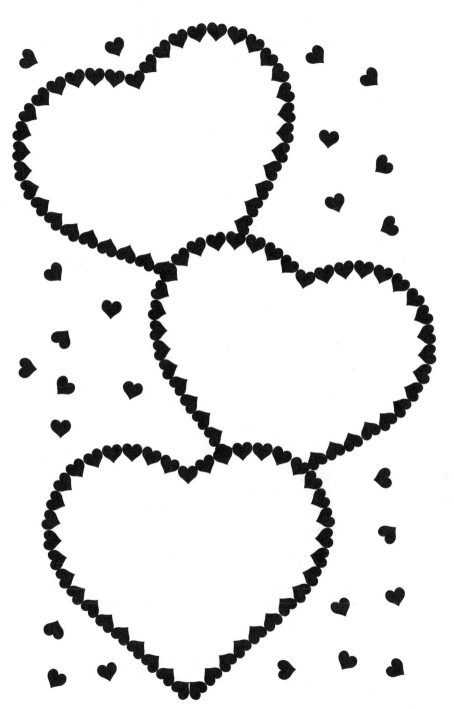

On Being Angry

When I'm angry God,
I feel like a steaming kettle of boiling water.
I feel that at any moment
my lid might pop right off.
When I'm angry,
sometimes I say things I don't mean.
But sometimes I'm angry
because someone is hurting someone else
and I want to make them stop.
God help me not to keep my anger inside,
but please help me
to calmly express my feelings.
Help me to be mature when I am angry.

What kinds of things make you angry? _____

_____

_____

How do you act when you are upset? _____

_____

_____

☞ Write a short prayer or thoughtful saying to recite every time
you get angry. Recite the prayer or saying before you express
your angry feelings. This should help you calm down before
you say something hurtful.

● PEACE ● PRAYER ● PEACE ● PRAYER ●

● PEACE ● PRAYER ● PEACE ● PRAYER ●

Feeling Silly

God, sometimes I'm in such a good mood
that I laugh and giggle and act really silly.
I think it's fun to act out a funny scene
or tell silly jokes or even just let go.
God, I'm thankful
for how carefree
and light-hearted I feel
when I'm in a
silly mood.
Thank you
for giving me
this wonderful
feeling!
Amen.

☞ Do you ever feel like you're in a silly mood? Make
a list of things you like to do when you are feeling
this way and write a short prayer thanking God
for the fun things on your list.

About
Loneliness

God, sometimes I feel
like no one can understand me
and I feel lonely.
My parents get busy sometimes
and sometimes my friends seem far away.
Sometimes there's just no one to talk to.
When I feel lonely, God,
please help me to remember
that you are always there for me.
I can talk to you
and you will always keep me company.
Thank you for always being there for me.

☞ Draw a picture of
yourself when you
feel lonely. Then draw
a picture of yourself
after you talk with
God about how you
are feeling.

When
I feel
lonely...

How
I feel
after I talk
to God
about my
loneliness...

Sharing

God, sharing something
with someone else always feels so good.
Whether I share my lunch cookies
with a friend,
or share my bike with my brother,
or even if I give some of my allowance
to the poor,
I always feel good afterwards.
At times, when I have something
that means a lot to me,
it's hard to share.
But when I do share, I'm always glad I did.
Help me to always have a good heart
and be generous with other people.
And thank you for all the times
people have shared with me.

What I shared today:

☞ As a prayer to God, make a special effort to share something with someone today. It doesn't have to be a big thing. Even small things that are shared can have great meaning.

Chapter 4

Prayers about Things that Happen in Our World

"Those who are generous are blessed,
for they share their bread
with the poor"
(Proverbs 22:9).

A Prayer
for the Homeless

I saw a homeless man today,
and in the rain is where he stayed
because he had no place to go.
I wondered what he did when it
snowed.

I heard a homeless woman say
"Can you spare some change today?"
No one looked her in the eye.
All the people passed her by.

I asked the homeless man today,
and the woman too, if they prayed?
"Yes, we do," the woman said.
"God gives us hope that we'll have
bread."

"But God helps us through kids like you.
And grown-ups who are caring, too.
So pray for us that God may see
a way for them to help people like me."

So every night I say some prayers
asking God to ease their cares.
And I give some allowance every week
to shelters who give them food to eat.

God helps homeless people through
caring people like me and you.

 Get together with your class or with your family to talk about ways you can help the homeless. You might want to take up a collection of clothes, have a bake sale or volunteer at a soup kitchen or a shelter with your class or family.

Put a photo here of you doing something to help homeless people.

Helping the homeless...

A Prayer about Schools and Learning

God, please help adults
and people in our government
to understand how important school is
to kids and our future.
Help them to find ways to improve education.
We need good books and computers,
and we need more teachers
who like to help kids learn.
Please help grown-ups to continue to care
about us kids and our education.
Amen.

☞ Write a letter to the President or Congress and your Governor and city leaders, letting them know how you feel about their support of schools and education. Let this be your prayer to God about education and schools.

Dear _____ ,

The Drug Problem

God, drugs scare me.
I know how bad it is to take drugs,
but a lot of kids take them
and I'm afraid they might hurt themselves
and other people, too.
It frightens me that people
have even been killed
because of drugs.
God, please help everyone to be strong
enough to stop this terrible problem.
And please help me not to be afraid
to speak out against drugs.

☞ Create an anti-drug slogan. Then design a jacket with special paints or markers with your slogan and a logo. Ask your friends or classmates to join in and design their own jackets, too.

Prejudice

I wish that people would use their eyes
to see beyond looks or size.
Some people don't think that it's a sin
to judge a person by the color of their skin.

But if inside a person is all we could see
the prejudice would no longer be,
because inside we're all the same
with a heart and soul and a special name.

God lives inside each one of us,
so we can show each other love and trust.

☞ Now write an original poem and express your feelings about prejudice. Your poem doesn't need to rhyme; just express what you feel.

On the Environment

Earth is such a beautiful place.
It is full of miracles and wonders.
But God, we aren't always so good
at taking care of the earth.
We have a lot of pollution
and we are cutting down too many trees.
We are sometimes wasteful
and even greedy with our natural resources.
Sometimes I am wasteful and greedy, too.
Please God, help us all
to take care of the earth
and protect its beauty.
If we take care of the earth,
the earth will take care of us.

☞ Get together with your classmates, friends or
family and create an "Earth Group." Talk
about what you can do as a group to take
care of the earth. You can start a recycling
program for your school, neighborhood or
family. You can plant trees or write letters to
government officials. Do this as your prayer to
God. Remember, it was God who created the
earth for us in the first place.

87

About Crime

I feel so sad when I hear about
the crime and violence in our society.
God, many people are hurting
because of the crimes that happen today.
Help us to respect ourselves
and other people.
Help us to help others learn
that stealing is sinful
and every human life is sacred.
God, help everyone to work together
to stop crime and violence in our country.
Amen.

☞ Now write an original prayer about
your concerns about crime and
violence in our society. What do
you think causes these problems?

My Prayer
about Crime

A Prayer for Our National Leaders

God, when you're a kid
you have to count on grown-ups
to make good decisions for you.
We have many politicians and leaders
who need your help in making decisions
every day.
Please guide the President (or Prime Minister)
and other world and national leaders
and give them strength to do what's right,
not just what is easy for people.
And help today's children to learn to be good
leaders for the future.

☞ Have your classmates, friends or family get together in small groups. Write down some major problems or issues facing the country, or your town or school. Put each issue into a hat. Then have each group pick an issue. Each group is then assigned the task of coming up with a solution to the problem and presenting the solution to the other groups.

ISSUES

91

Chapter 5

Prayers about
All Kinds of Things

"God saw everything that He had made,
and indeed, it was very good"
(Genesis 1:31).

Help
with
Solving
a
Problem

God, I need your help
with a problem that's really tough.
I don't know what to do
and all this worry is getting rough.

I believe that you know everything
and you'll help me find the way,
to solve this great big problem
that's in my way today.

I know the answer will come
because I have faith in you.
And I ask just one more thing:
Help me follow the answer through.

☞ Do you have a pressing problem or just something you
can't solve? It could be a big or small problem or maybe
just a tricky situation. Pick a problem with which you
would like God's help. Then find some quiet time and
write to God about the problem and what some of the
solutions might be. Remain as peaceful as you can and
have faith that God will guide you to the best solution.

On Judging Other People

Lord, I want to always keep
these words of Scripture in mind:
"Do not judge, so that you may not be judged"
(Matthew 7:1).

Please keep me away from the temptation
of being too critical of other people.
Help me to remember that the people in my
life, including the adults, are only human.

☞ Now, in your own words, write a prayer to
God about judgment. Include your desire
to treat other people gently in your
thoughts and deeds.

Asking for Forgiveness

Dear God, I want to ask
for your forgiveness.
I did something that I knew was wrong.
I went against your teachings
and I am very sorry.
I know that asking forgiveness
means these things:

- I must feel really sorry in my heart for what I did and ask your forgiveness.

- I must make things right with any person hurt and tell them I am sorry.

- Then I must forgive myself and remember not to do this again.

God, help me to be strong
when I am tempted
to do something against you.
With your help,
I will be a kind and loving person always.

☞ Take some time to be quiet and alone with God. Talk to God about something for which you need to be forgiven. Everybody does some things they wish they hadn't, so don't feel like you are alone. Tell God how you feel. Then think of something kind you can do for someone else or for a person you may have hurt. Kindness is a wonderful way of healing hurts and showing that you are truly sorry.

Some kind things I can do for people I have hurt:

_____   _____
_____   _____
_____   _____
_____   _____
_____   _____
_____   _____
_____   _____
_____   _____

When You Make a Mistake

God, when I make a mistake
I don't always like to admit it.
It's hard to know that I could have done better
at my schoolwork or on the team.
And sometimes I don't make
the right decisions
when I have to make a choice.
I even get angry at myself
when I make mistakes.
I feel embarrassed, too.
Please help me to know
that it's okay to make mistakes,
and that I can learn from them.
I know that you understand
that part of growing and learning
means making mistakes.
Help me to understand this, too.

☞ Have you ever made a mistake and felt embarrassed
or upset about it? As your prayer to God, write down
what you think *God* would say to you about your
mistake. Remember that God's loving and gentle
and wants to help all of us to learn.

Growing Up with One Parent

I am asking for some special help, God.
As you know, I only have one parent.
Most of the other kids have two.
This is pretty hard on me
and it's hard on my parent sometimes, too.
Could you look after us with a little extra care?
Make sure we aren't lonely
and that we remember
that we are still a family,
even if it's a different kind of family.
Help me not to feel jealous
of some of the other kids
because they have two parents.
Amen.

☞ If you have only one parent, what special circum-
stances does this create for you? What is unique
about your family life? What are the good things and
some of the difficult things about having only one
parent? Now write to God about your family life and
ask for the things you need to strengthen you.

Put a photo of you and
your family here.

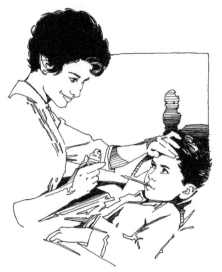

A Get Well Wish for Someone You Love

God, I know someone who is very sick
and needs your help to feel better
and be healed.
I love them very much
and I am asking you to show them
your love, too.
Please God, hear my prayers
and help them get well as soon as possible.

☞ Now offer a get well wish for a sick relative or friend
in your own words. Tell God why this person is
important to you and what his/her recovery means
to you. Then make a get well card for the person
who is ill. Let them know you are praying for them.
Your heartfelt prayers will be important to them.

CARD PRACTICE SHEET

FRONT   BACK

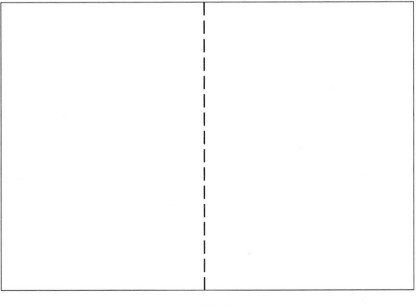

INSIDE

When a Grandparent Dies

Oh God,
this is the hardest kind of
prayer I can think of.
It hurts so much to lose my grandparent.
I miss my grandparent like anything.
It's hard for me to accept
that my grandparent isn't here anymore.
I know that I cannot understand all your ways
but I know you have a reason for everything—
even dying.
I know "there is a time
for every matter under heaven" (Ecclesiastes
3:1). But please look after my grandparents
and make sure they have a place in heaven.
Please tell my grandparents how I'm doing
and that I miss them.
Amen.

☞ Have you lost a grandparent? Write down some things that you
would like to say to your grandparent. Then write a prayer to
God and talk about this difficult experience. You may wish to
include all the things that you love about your grandparent and
share your letter with your parents.

What I would like to say to my grandparent:

A Graduation Prayer

This is a special day
so I want to say in a special way,
thank you, Lord, for all I've learned,
for all my friends and the grades I've earned;
for my helpful teachers
and hard work I've done,
and for all the memories
that were so much fun.
As I grow and go on in school,
please stay close and guide me through.

☞ Before the graduation ceremony or soon
after, take some special time out to let
God know you're thinking of him at this
important time of growth and change.
You can do this by saying or writing a
prayer or by making a list of things you
want to thank God for regarding your
school years and graduation.

A Prayer for a Safe Journey or Vacation

God, as you know, we're going on a trip.
Please look after us and make sure we are
safe from harm or injury.
Allow us to enjoy our traveling
and thank you for giving us the chance to see
new places
and visit friends and family.
Help me to take time on our journey
to thank you for all the blessings
you have given us.
Amen.

☞ Write your own prayer to God about a future
trip that you are about to take, or maybe just
one you would like to embark on someday.

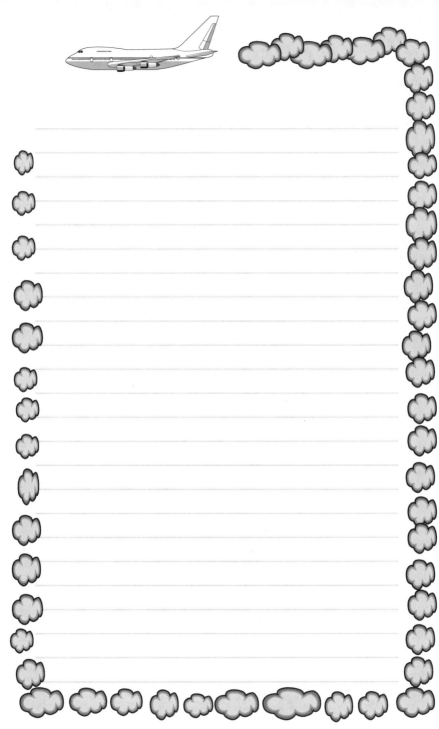

Love for a Pet

Thank you, God, for my wonderful pet!
I love him so much.
My pet is like a friend to me
and we have a lot of fun together.
I feel like my pet is a part of the family.
Sometimes when I'm lonely,
I remember that my pet is there for me,
and that helps me a lot.
Help me always to take good care of my pet
to show my love.

☞ Now draw a picture of your pet. On the bottom of
the page, write a short prayer to God concerning
your pet. Say whatever is in your heart.

When a Pet Dies

God, my pet died.
He was like a
best friend to me.
I'm so sad I feel like crying.
God, I don't understand
why he had to die
and where he has gone.
I feel so upset, God.
Wherever my pet is,
God, let him know
that I love him
and miss him.
And God,
please help me
to understand more
about life
and help me not to feel
so sad.

👉 Have you lost a pet? What did you feel when your pet died?
Where do you imagine your pet went when he died? In remembrance of your pet, make a mobile. Draw pictures of your pet
and God taking care of your pet. You can draw pictures of you
with your pet, too. Then cut out the pictures and glue a piece of
string to the back of each one. Tie the strings on a hanger (you
can cover the hanger with material or felt if you wish) and hang
your mobile where it will be a nice reminder of your pet.

My Pet Mobile

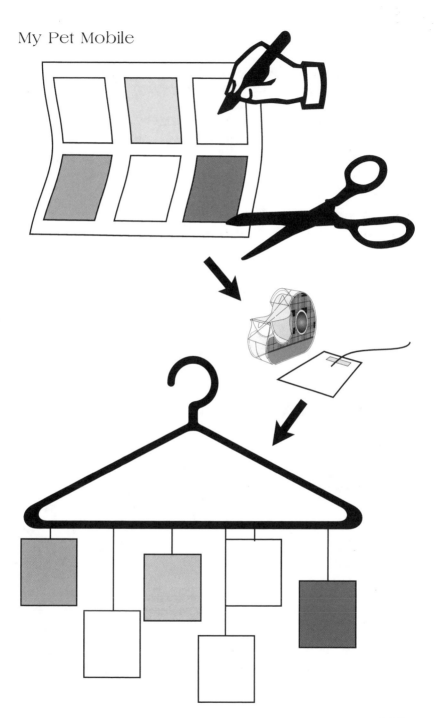

About Playing Sports

Dear God, please make sure
I don't get hurt playing sports
and make sure that nobody else does either.
Help me to play my hardest and try my best,
but guide me so I play fair, too.
And most of all,
I promise to remember that games
are meant for fun.
Thank you for helping me be part of the team.

☞ Do you like to play sports on a team or in a gym class? Draw a
picture of God helping you play your favorite sport. What do
you think God thinks about athletics?

About the Bible

The Bible is a wonderful book, God.
Both the Old and the New Testament
are very interesting and full of wisdom.
I know that a person can learn so much
about life and about you, God,
through reading and studying the Bible.
Thank you for this great gift of knowledge
and hope for us all.

☞ Do you have your own Bible? If not, remember that nearly all
public libraries have them. Cut out a piece of cardboard,
construction paper, or poster board in the shape of a bookmark.
Then select your favorite Bible passage and print it on the
bookmark. You can also illustrate your new bookmark with a
scene from the Bible if you like. You can even copy some of
your favorite Bible verses on small sheets of paper and make a
little booklet and read the quotes whenever you feel like making
a little prayer to God.

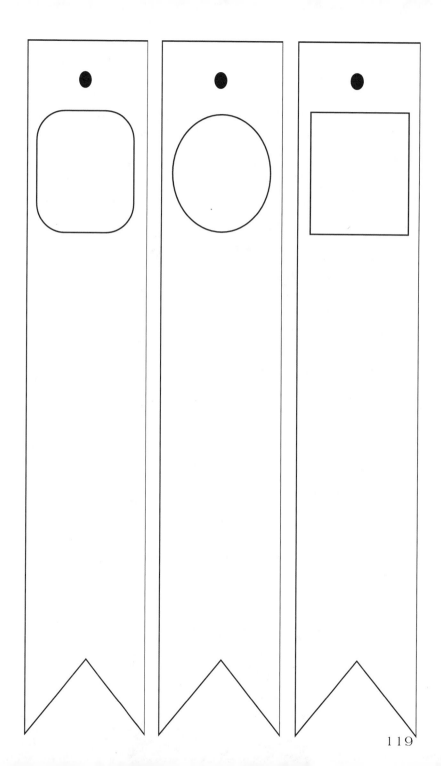

Chapter 6

Prayers about Holidays and Special Times

"Glory to God in the highest heaven,
and on earth peace among
those whom he favors"

(Luke 2:14).

A Birthday Prayer

God, it's my birthday!
Thank you for giving me my own special day
to celebrate life!
Please help me in this next year of my life
to learn new things
and to appreciate all the blessings
you have given me.
I really want to be the best person I can be.
Thank you for my family and friends
and for the special things they do for me
all year long.
God, thanks for giving me the gift of life.

☞ Now make a birthday card from you to you! In it, write down what you want to do to show God how thankful you are for the life that you have.

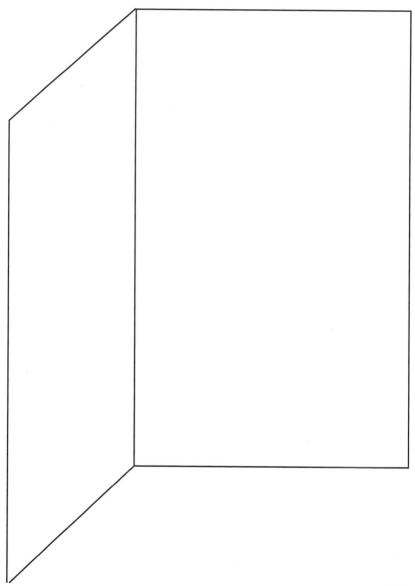

A Prayer for the New Year

Happy New Year, God!
New Year's Eve is always a time
when I like to think about all the things
I did in the year—
the good things and the not so good things.
I like to take the time to decide
how I'm going to improve myself
in the next year.
Then I like to throw confetti and have fun!
Thank you for all your help
in the past year, God.
And please help me
always to grow closer to you
and to be a more religious person
each and every day of the New Year!
Amen.

☞ Make a list of twelve things you want to do in the New Year.
Think about what you want to improve in your life. Write all
these things down and ask God to look after you as you try to
keep your resolutions during the New Year.

A Prayer for Martin Luther King Day

God, it is such a sad thing
that Martin Luther King, Jr. was assassinated.
I am thankful that his life brought about
so much hope and change for all of us.
But there is still prejudice today,
and we all need to keep working hard
so all people will be treated
with equal justice.
Please God, help every person realize
that we are all your children
and we are all equal in your eyes.
We are truly brothers and sisters.
Amen.

☞ Go to the library and find a book on the life of Martin Luther King, Jr. Read about the things he tried to accomplish. Then make a list of some things you can do every day to help get rid of prejudice in our world.

For Valentine's Day

God, it is so wonderful
to have a day just to celebrate love.
Love is so important.
Without love, nothing really matters.
I love you, God.
And I know that you love me.
I learned a lot about love
from the Bible, too.
I learned that your love
has no limits.
Thank you for this day
to allow me to openly express
my love for my family
and friends.
Amen.

☞ Read Chapter 13 of 1 Corinthians in your Bible. Then on a nice piece of paper write down *your* ideas about what love is. Draw some pictures around your words and give yourself this Valentine to remind yourself about love every day.

For Presidents' Day

We have had many Presidents, God.
And all of them had a hard job to do.
Help me to remember
that these people worked hard to help the
United States.
Today I want to thank you
for the good things they have done
and to ask you to help the current President to do
a good job
and to take care of our country
and our citizens.
Amen.

☞ Think of a slogan to describe the importance of President's Day and the office of President of the United States. Write the slogan on a T-shirt, gym shoes, shorts or just on paper. Decorate your item in red, white and blue.

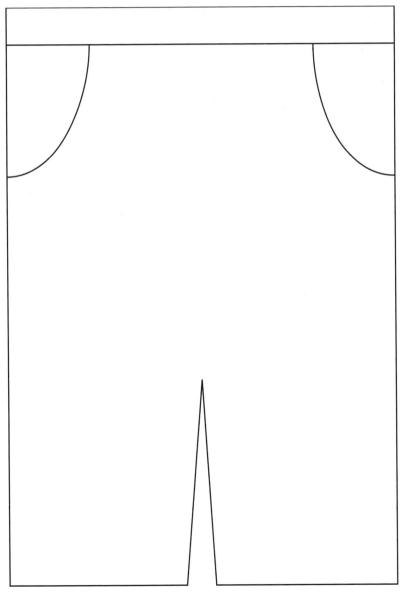

An Easter/ Springtime Prayer

God, spring is such a beautiful
time of year.
Everything is new and alive.
The trees and flowers bloom
and there are ducklings and calves
and baby chicks being born.
It's really a season of hope
and new life.
Thank you for giving us Easter
and for its powerful message of hope,
life and renewal.
I know that Jesus came
to bring new life.
I want to learn more about this
as I grow up.
So thank you for making
this special holiday.

 Write an original prayer to God and express your
feelings about Easter and springtime or create
separate prayers for each.

About the Fourth of July

God, every 4th of July
fireworks burst and freedom rings!
We have picnics and barbecues and enjoy the
summer sun.
Especially on this holiday,
we thank you for the goodness and freedom
we have in our country.
Help us never to take our freedom for
granted.
And most of all,
I pray for all the people in the world
who do not know the joys of freedom.

☞ Now write a poem about the 4th of July and express
your feelings about the meaning of freedom. Share
your poem with God and members of your family.

Halloween

This year, God,
I am going to have extra fun at Halloween
by doing something for others.
I would like to have a costume party
for my friends and classmates.
The theme would be to dress up like your
favorite hero.
We'd have lots of candy,
and we'd carve pumpkins and drink hot apple
cider.
We could even make Halloween favors
for the senior citizens in our town.
We could visit them in our costumes,
so they could have a fun Halloween, too!
Maybe I won't really be able to do these
things,
but please, God, show me something I *can* do
for a safe and happy Halloween.

☞ What do you usually do for Halloween? This year, as your prayer to God, think of something you can also do for someone else. Talk to your parents or teacher about helping you with this project. Involve as many friends, neighbors and classmates as you can. You can even make a scrapbook of the event by taking pictures and writing about it.

Prayer for Thanksgiving

Big orange pumpkins,
Turkey with stuffing,
Pecan pie and pumpkin pie,
Warm sweaters and cold wind,
A crackling fire in the hearth,
Family,
Friends,
Laughter and Sharing.
Thanksgiving.

God, you give us so much to be thankful for—
our rich history and our modern advantages.
Especially at Thanksgiving
we remember how good you are to us
and how you always provide us
with the things that we need.
Help us always to share
our abundance with others.

☞ Write your own prayer
    of thanksgiving to
    God. You may wish to
    ask your parents if you
    may read your prayer
    as a blessing before
    the Thanksgiving
    meal.

A Christmas Prayer

Christmas is not only about buying gifts
and tinsel and decorations.
Christmas is about love.
When Jesus was born
he represented peace and hope
and God's love for the world.
God, help us to remember
the true meaning of Christmas.
Help us to give of ourselves.
Thank you for the special warm feelings
that we all have around Christmas.
Please bless the people who are lonely
or who feel left out at Christmas time.
Let them feel your love, God.
Christmas is for everyone.

☞ Make a list of people for whom you would normally buy Christmas presents. Instead of buying a gift, next to each person's name write down something you will do for them. For example: you could take your brother's turn to wash dishes one day, or donate canned goods to a food pantry in someone else's name. Make a card for each person and tell them in your original card what you wish to give them for Christmas.

Name: What I will do
                      for them:

About the Authors

David Heller, Ph.D. is a leading authority on children and their views of religion and the world. He has authored a number of successful books on the subject, including *Just Build the Ark and The Animals Will Come; Love is Like a Crayon Because It Comes in All Colors; Talking to Your Child about God; Dear God: Children's Letters to God; The Children's God;* and *Growing Up Isn't Hard If You Start Out As a Kid.* His work with children has been featured all across the country, including segments on "20/20" and CNBC, and articles in *People, Parents, Good Housekeeping, Catholic Digest, Redbook, USA Today, Psychology Today, Parenting* and in nationally syndicated pieces for Universal Press Syndicate. He graduated from Harvard and the University of Michigan, and has taught at both as well.

Elizabeth Heller, M.S. has assisted on all the previously mentioned books and has co-authored *The Best Christmas Presents Are Wrapped in Heaven* and *Grandparents Are Made for Hugging.* One of her great loves is writing poetry for children. She has developed a children's news program for cable TV and produced and hosted a radio show for children on WBZ in Boston. Elizabeth has also served as Director of Public Relations for Catholic Charities. She holds a bachelor's degree in English from Santa Clara and a master's degree in Journalism.